Biblical Patterns for Powerful Church Prayer Meetings

God's Changeless Path to Sweeping Revival and Evangelism

Discover How Any Church Can Experience God in Corporate and Small Group Prayer Meetings!

Dr. Gregory R. Frizzell

Biblical Patterns for Powerful Church Prayer Meetings
ISBN 0-9665424-3-6

Copyright © 1999 by Gregory R. Frizzell
Published by The Master Design
 789 State Route 94 E
 Fulton, KY 42041
 www.masterdesign.org

All rights reserved. No part of this publication may be reproduced, stored in a retrieval system or transmitted in any way by any means, electronic, mechanical, photocopy, recording or otherwise, without the prior permission of the author, except as provided by USA copyright law.

Unless otherwise noted, Scripture quotations are from the KING JAMES VERSION AV of the Bible © 1973, Thomas Nelson, Inc., Publishers.

Printed by Bethany Press International in the USA.

Foreword

This little booklet is a most timely and crucial tool for every pastor and every church! Just the reading of it will quicken the heart to pursue, with all earnestness, immediate obedience in corporate prayer before God.

It cost God the life of His Son to provide access to "enter the holiest" (Hebrews 10:19,20), so the heart of God urges us "...to draw near with a true heart in full assurance of faith" (Hebrews 10:22).

Especially in the New Testament, God's absolute 'essential' for His Presence and Power to radically change lives, cities, and whole nations, is believing, obedient, *corporate prayer*! The churches were devoted to their Lord and therefore to corporate prayer, and experienced God's mighty activity as they prayed. They knew they were "workers together with God" (2 Corinthians 6:1,2). Every time of prayer was a crucial time before God. God guided, directed and empowered them all.

History now bears witness to revival and awakening that "turned the world upside down" (Acts 17:6), with countless multitudes being saved. Some of my own fondest memories growing up were the intense and long (often 2 hours) corporate prayer meetings in our home. Some of my deepest recollections in my almost 30 years as a pastor are the midweek prayer meetings. And some of my most sacred times were praying for my missionary uncle and aunt in Northern China, and hearing the reports of the great and historic Shantung Revival.

Now it is our turn! The witness is before us! The decision awaits us! Heaven is anticipating our obedience, and waiting to burst into celebration over every believer, and every unbeliever who repents (Luke 15:7,10,22-24).

May we join together, week after week, in corporate, power-filled *prayer meetings*! God will receive great glory as we use this little booklet, born in the heart of a pastor, to see every church become a "house of prayer."

Henry T. Blackaby

Introduction

It is with a profound sense of excitement and awe that I took the assignment to write this resource. On one hand there is great excitement about today's rapidly growing prayer movement. God is up to something truly miraculous! Yet, there must also be deep concern for society's moral decline. No doubt we are all burdened by America's catastrophic moral collapse. In fact, if present moral trends continue, it is hard to imagine the conditions we soon will face. Perhaps the psalmist said it best. *"If the foundations be destroyed, what can the righteous do?"* (Psalms 11:3)

Beyond question, the need for revival has become desperate and we can no longer merely hope for a few percentage points of baptism increase. If America is to reverse its devastating decline, we must again see the four and five hundred percent baptism increases of some past Great Awakenings. Thank God, He has so touched nations before and can certainly do so again! Yet, biblically and historically, there is only one way God ever sends such massive evangelistic floods. *That one way is powerful corporate prayer meetings combined with intense evangelistic passion!*

In spite of society's darkness, I write with a growing sense of excitement and hope. Indeed some churches are returning to corporate prayer and a new evangelistic passion. We should be much encouraged by the rapid spread of the FAITH Sunday School Strategy and other excellent evangelistic tools. Clearly, God is laying foundations for a potential explosion of evangelism and missions!

It is my earnest prayer that every pastor will embrace FAITH, Continuing Witnessing Training, People Sharing Jesus or some effective tool for reaching the lost. Yet history proves that strategies alone can never bring the huge spiritual floods that shake whole nations. According to scripture, if a major awakening is to come, evangelistic efforts must be accompanied by a massive return to God through fervent prayer and deep repentance. (2 Chronicles 7:14; Jeremiah 29:13; James 5:16) There is hope that at least for some, this is beginning to happen!

In recent years we increasingly hear the term "prayer evangelism." (Prayer evangelism is the intentional effort to saturate all evangelistic strategies with far greater levels of prayer.) In prayer evangelism, prayer actually becomes the foundational strategy rather than merely one of many side ingredients. Prayer walking, prayer journeys and lighthouses of prayer are enjoying rapid growth among God's people. Yet, perhaps most encouraging is the number of pastors who are asking, *"How can I truly reclaim Wednesday nights as a time of powerful, prayer for evangelism, missions and revival?"*

In addition to pastors, state leaders are asking for biblical ways to unite whole conventions as "houses of prayer." In July of 1999, I was led to propose a major resolution and strategy for four Wednesday nights of prayer across many state conventions. Almost immediately, eight states adopted the prayer resolution and at least eight other states are now in the process! In our lifetime, we have not witnessed such eagerness to return to God through corporate prayer.

This resource was birthed from a burning passion to see churches embrace dynamic prayer meetings. Beyond question, corporate prayer is the foundational pattern in nearly all great revivals of history. Though a variety of prayer strategies are certainly important, none can rival the historic role of the *corporate* prayer meeting. (Acts 1:14; 2:1,42; 4:24,31; 6:4) Indeed, no prayer strategy can fully substitute for powerful church-wide prayer.

Many readers may be shocked to discover how far churches have drifted from historic patterns of vibrant corporate prayer. At the same time, all will be encouraged by simple biblical patterns through which God will revolutionize the prayer meeting of any church. *Pastor, please believe that your church can reclaim the mighty power of the church-wide prayer meeting!* In this resource, we will examine biblical ways it can be done without neglecting any ministry activities or organizations.

Having pastored in a difficult, high crime setting for over fifteen years, I write as a "fellow learner" and *not* as one with all the answers. Far from trying to lecture my fellow pastors, I humbly share that with which God has deeply convicted and challenged my own heart. Though my church is certainly not perfect in all areas of prayer, what we have discovered has made an astounding difference! According to God's promise, He will mightily bless *any* church that returns to Him in serious corporate prayer. (Matthew 7:7)

Friends, in spite of deep spiritual darkness, there are glorious signs God is doing a phenomenal new work. Recently, the stage has been set with tremendous tools for discipleship, evangelism and missions. But even more, we are seeing some churches return to God in corporate prayer and humility. Could it be that we may at last *combine* our strategies with fervent prayer? Today we are blessed with denominational leaders who truly want this to happen. We are also blessed with excellent new tools for a variety of prayer strategies. (See LifeWay and NAMB resources listed at the back.)

Before closing this introduction, I must emphasize that strong prayer meetings are not about particular formats, programs or events. At its heart, a genuine prayer meeting is a glorious *relationship encounter* with Christ Himself! Prayer is a by-product of your love relationship with the Lord.

As you read the coming chapters, please ask God to speak personally to your heart. My passion is not to promote a concept, but to instill a heart hunger for a new relationship with God Himself. This resource is actually a small synopsis of the much larger book, *A Comprehensive Guide to Church and Small Group Prayer Meetings.* (For far more detailed help on prayer meetings, see the resources in the back.)

May God help us see that powerful corporate prayer is *essential* to a mighty move of God in our day. According to Ezekiel 22:30, God expects us to stand in the gap and friends, this can only happen *if* we truly become a house of prayer. (Mark 11:17) May God save us from the deadly tendency to major on programs while only minoring on prayer. Above all, let us stand in the glorious faith that God can still shake our land for His glory. To Him alone be glory, honor and praise!

Toward the Next Great Awakening,

Gregory R. Frizzell

Chapter One
Powerful Church Prayer Meetings
America's Most Desperate Need

In view of America's shocking spiritual decline, the title of this chapter may seem hopelessly simplistic. Indeed, with society's staggering problems, how could powerful prayer meetings represent our most desperate need? Yet according to scripture and history, that is unquestionably the case. (2 Chronicles 7:14) To put it simply, there has practically never been a massive spiritual awakening until churches first returned to God in powerful corporate prayer meetings. On the other hand, every time churches did return to deep prayer and humility, God shook the land for His glory!

At this point, I again stress what is meant by the term "powerful church prayer meeting." I am not referring to certain methods or formats. Neither do I mean merely an event to orchestrate. *A genuine prayer meeting is nothing less than a powerful, relationship encounter with God Himself.* When past generations embraced church prayer meetings as a life-changing relationship with God, they soon experienced a phenomenal outpouring of His presence. As they learned to approach God in genuine prayer and repentance, their ministry efforts took on nation-shaking power!

Though it sounds incredibly simple, corporate prayer is God's primary pattern for sweeping evangelism and revival. When past generations returned to God in fervent prayer, they quickly discovered He had not lost His power to transform a sinful society. But what caused earlier generations to place such intense focus on seeking God through prayer?

First, they had a deep belief that intense corporate prayer was "essential" to meeting God in revival and widespread evangelism. Earlier generations believed God would use prayer to make a profound difference in their cities. They believed if enough churches united in fervent prayer, God would reveal His mighty presence. They were also convinced God would not send a spiritual awakening without corporate prayer and repentance. Because of such convictions, powerful prayer meetings became a major priority. Furthermore, these generations hungered for a new relationship with God, and not merely for His outward blessing. They fully understood that the church's true power could not be measured by the brilliance of its programs but by the depth of its prayer meetings!

Second, earlier generations were experienced at meeting God in powerful prayer meetings. They viewed prayer meetings as life-changing encounters with God and not just brief devotional services. Furthermore, their meetings were not so rigidly bound to brief time schedules. They truly understood how to meet God in life-changing prayer. As you study the prayer patterns from past awakenings, you will notice a striking difference from typical meetings today. Sadly, many modern prayer meetings bear little resemblance to the spontaneity, fervency, or evangelistic focus of meetings from the revival generations.

Third, former generations exhibited intense spiritual hunger and a deep desperation to seek God's face in prayer. A sense of urgency drove them to prayer as a major top priority. Because of a deep feeling of need, they felt they had no choice but to embrace powerful corporate prayer meetings. Their desperation drove them to the belief that no program could ever substitute for fervent church-wide prayer. They believed God would send revival if (and only if) they sought Him with "extraordinary" prayer. (Jeremiah 29:13, "And you shall seek me, and find me, when you shall search for me with all your heart.")

This brings us to two crucial questions. Are today's churches truly desperate about America's moral collapse? Is there desperation about the lack of spiritual vitality and growing worldliness in so many churches? An honest assessment of modern prayer meetings suggests that most are not desperate for God. Yet, society has indeed reached a point of extreme spiritual emergency. Friends, if there was ever a time we should be desperate, that time is now! In fact, after twenty years of studying historic patterns, I am prepared to state we are in the worst moral collapse of America's history. Even as little as five years ago, I could not make that statement. Yet in view of recent trends, I must make that statement!

In a few short years, our nation has crossed unprecedented thresholds of moral perversion. At an alarming rate, gross perversion and wickedness are increasingly exalted as "good" while the righteous are depicted as "intolerant" and "evil." (Isaiah 5:20)

We must awaken to the fact that something very unusual is happening in our nation. What we are witnessing is not just a cyclical rise and fall of morals! America is in a huge spiritual crisis and we cannot afford to major on programs and while merely minoring on prayer meetings. According to scripture, the only hope for revival is a widespread return to the intense prayer patterns of the early church and the revival generations. If you still have any doubt about the urgency of our situation, prayerfully consider some recent signs of a desperate spiritual crisis.

Eight Signs of Spiritual Emergency

(1) *During the last forty years, every form of immorality has witnessed an unprecedented explosion.*[1] Practices such as adultery, divorce, incest, premarital sex, homosexuality, suicide and abortion have risen at an astounding rate. Divorce rates are by far the highest in the so-called bible belt. There is now a tenfold increase in numbers of couples living together outside of wedlock! In major cities, illegitimacy rates have exploded anywhere from five hundred to more than one thousand percent. Such rapid moral and family disintegration is among the most extreme in human history. Few nations have ever changed so radically in such a short period of time. (And in so-called "Christian" America.)

(2) *Since 1960 nearly every category of crime has risen by the alarming ratio of four to five hundred percent.*[2] Most senior adults easily remember a time when few people locked their doors. Yet, today society lives barricaded behind steel bars and security systems. Again, this rapid rate of crime growth is rare in human history. Though recently some crime has shown a slight decrease, society remains at catastrophic levels of criminal activity. Perhaps most alarming is the huge explosion of violent crime among children and youth.

(3) *An unprecedented combination of cultural forces exert strong anti-Christian influence on societal attitudes.* Powerful entertainment and music industries shamelessly promote a constant message that is anti-moral, anti-Bible and anti-Christ.[3] Many public and higher education systems have evolved into powerful forces against God and the biblical foundations of our nation. History books have been "revised" to eliminate nearly all references to the Christian foundations of our country. Never have so many forces "combined" to alter the moral mind set of a society.

For most of today's children, their primary exposure to Jesus is the blatant anti-Christian bias from Hollywood, music industries, news media and secularized education. Perversion and immorality are highly exalted and "normalized" while Christians are constantly depicted as "intolerant bigots." (If we think it is difficult to evangelize Americans now, wait until today's indoctrinated youth reach adulthood!)

(4) *During the 1990's, we have witnessed an alarming rise in hostility against Christians and biblical values.* Fifteen years ago few comedians would even mildly joke about the church, yet today open blasphemy is the constant theme of actors, comedians and talk show hosts.[4] Today Christians are just about the only group that can be slandered with impunity. In "Christian" America, we are rapidly reaching the place where it must be said, "There is no fear of God in the land." Never has there been an American generation so hostile to the teachings of God's Word. At an alarming rate, modern Christians are being demonized by secular society. People who in any way take biblical morality seriously are now called the "radical" right.

(5) *Laws presently proposed could eventually make it a federal crime to espouse the biblical view of homosexuality.* (Such laws already exist in Canada.) Highly organized homosexual groups stand poised to use such laws to sue churches and potentially jail ministers.

Other proposed laws, if passed, would totally reverse the biblical definition of marriage in America. At present, some states are incredibly close to passing such a law. Increasing numbers of communities move ever closer to outlawing door to door evangelism. Whether or not we realize it, American Christians are moving close to significant forms of legal oppression.

(6) *During the last twenty years, America has experienced a massive explosion of cults and false religions.* Astrology, psychics and Satanism are growing at unprecedented rates. Religions such as Islam and New Age cults are growing at phenomenal rates. By contrast, it is estimated that each year three to four thousand American churches close their doors for the last time. At present, the percentage growth of cults and false religions far outpace the growth of the nation's churches.

(7) *Despite history's biggest expansion of evangelistic programs and strategies, domestic baptism numbers for Southern Baptists have been essentially flat-lined for nearly fifty years.* (In spite of the fact that our national population has exploded!) These statistics actually mean "baptism ratios" have been in a serious fifty year decline. It is significant that this ratio decline has occurred during history's biggest increase of evangelistic programs, promotion and personnel. Despite a plethora of new programs and strategies, over seventy percent of our churches are

either plateaued or declining! The same or worse statistics are true of most evangelical denominations. These facts strongly suggest that the primary answer cannot be merely a better program or strategy.

(8) *Most years, well over fourteen thousand Southern Baptist churches baptize three or less, with seven to eight thousand actually baptizing no one!*[5] Over the last twenty years, thousands of our churches have declined so severely that they now barely cling to existence. Unless God intervenes in an awesome way, many thousands of these churches are projected to close within ten years. Furthermore, present church starts do not keep up with the population increase or with projected church closures.

Dear friend, in light of these alarming trends, you may be tempted to ask, "Is there any real hope for a great revival?" Let me state loud and clear, there is hope! God has miraculously changed our nation before and He can certainly do it again! (Hebrews 13:8) However, our hope must be nothing less than a miraculous spiritual awakening which far surpasses anything we have seen in our lifetime. (The last "statistically" significant nationwide awakening was in 1905.) We simply must see an awakening comparable to God's mighty movements of past centuries.

Praise God there are hopeful signs for a new day of evangelism and prayer. We should be deeply grateful for the strategies God is using mightily! We can take real encouragement in the development of excellent new evangelism strategies (such as FAITH) that are showing unique promise. But even more, we should take hope because growing numbers are returning to God through serious prayer! More and more churches are beginning to get serious about combining evangelism strategies with fervent prayer.

Before I describe the practical ways we can join the churches returning to prayer, it is crucial to understand "why" we left prayer in the first place. Indeed, two questions are key. (a) How did the world's most Christian nation get in its present spiritual condition? (b) With the development of Christianity's greatest programs, funding and strategies, how could society have fallen so far so fast? Though there are many reasons, certainly among the greatest is the drastic decline of church-wide prayer meetings and genuine discipleship.

In the midst of the explosion of ministry programs, we somehow forgot that God always requires intense prayer to release His mighty presence.

(Jeremiah 29:13, James 5:16) In the midst of so many "good" ministries and strategies, churches began to neglect the "best." It is obvious that congregations believed organizations and programs could substitute for deep humility and fervent corporate prayer meetings. Though it is sad to admit, dynamic biblical prayer meetings have long since disappeared from most of today's churches. Beyond question, the loss of corporate prayer has had profound negative impact on the power of the modern church.

Twentieth Century's Greatest Loss

The twentieth century was one of phenomenal advance in every area of life. During the last fifty years, Southern Baptists have enjoyed unprecedented expansion in evangelism programs, specialized personnel, and increased funding. Today, we have far more methods and strategies than ever. Modern believers have endless options for involvement in church activities. Yet during this same period of massive program expansion, something happened to most midweek prayer meetings. For all intents and purposes they ceased to be prayer meetings! Though the name remained the same, the practice changed dramatically. Unfortunately, most modern believers do not realize just how much our prayer meetings have changed. It is very important that we come to fully understand from "whence we have fallen."

As we study historic patterns from the New Testament and great awakening eras, we notice very distinct patterns in earlier church prayer meetings. Interestingly enough, these same patterns were fairly common for the first three hundred years of our own Baptist history. (During which time there were three great awakenings!) *So what were the historic patterns of corporate prayer and how have we changed from generations of great revival and evangelism?* The following patterns reveal a major shift from biblical and historic practices of church prayer meetings.

Powerful Prayer Patterns from Past Generations

(1) *In generations of great revivals, prayer meetings were focused mostly on prayers for lost people, personal repentance, revival, and mission initiatives.* Past prayer meetings focused primary attention on the key kingdom issues of evangelism, missions and sweeping revival.[6] (This pattern was especially true of generations that experienced great spiritual awakenings.) By contrast, modern meetings focus mostly on a brief prayer for a hospital list. Evangelism,

missions and personal repentance have long since ceased to be the predominant focus of most prayer meetings.

(2) *Until the twentieth century, prayer meetings were often led by lay people.*[7] Lay people were the primary prayer leaders and congregational participation was extensive. In past generations, congregations were participants and not merely spectators. By contrast, modern meetings are led mostly by the pastor and congregational participation is often minimal at best. (The point is not so much who leads the meeting, but how much the congregation participates.)

(3) *In past prayer meetings, people spent the majority of time actually praying.*[8] Little time was given for devotional sermons or talking "about" requests. The people came to talk to God. By contrast, modern prayer meetings typically consist of devotions and singing with only a tiny percentage of time given to direct communication with God. Actual prayer is often the least thing done at today's prayer meetings. By the time churches finish with announcements, singing, devotions and "talking about" prayer requests, almost no time is left for prayer.

(4) *Prayer meetings were not confined to brief time slots or crowded into the midst of many other activities.*[9] Revival generations promoted corporate prayer as the major church-wide experience. Because they believed prayer was important, the whole church typically spent an hour or more in fervent intercession for a variety of kingdom issues.

By contrast, most modern churches schedule many activities at the same time as prayer and split congregations into many different groups. Quite frequently, the prayer meeting is the least promoted (and least attended) of all church activities. In most churches, there is no such thing as a "church-wide" prayer meeting. In fact, in many churches, there is no prayer meeting at all.

(5) *Historically, church prayer meetings often involved whole families (including older children and youth).* As did the adults, children and youth learned the power of prayer by personal participation. In fact, revival generations valued the participation of young people. They understood that youth best learn to pray by actually praying and hearing others pray. They also understood that God hears the prayers of children and youth!

By contrast, today's youth are routinely excluded from prayer meetings. It has been all too common for children and youth to grow up in a Baptist church and never experience a corporate prayer meeting. (No wonder so many in today's generation see little value in church-wide corporate prayer.)

(6) *Historic church prayer meetings often contained strong emphasis on personal repentance and confession.* Pastors frequently shared scriptures that dealt with personal sin and called for specific prayers of repentance.[10] In the prayer meetings, people often confessed sin and asked others to pray for them in matters of spiritual struggle. (James 5:16) They believed spiritual cleansing was essential to whether God would ultimately hear their prayers. (Psalms 66:18) By contrast, personal confession and repentance are seldom a part of modern prayer meetings.

(7) *Fasting was a frequent emphasis in past prayer meetings.* For the first three hundred years of Baptist history, fasting was a rather common emphasis among serious believers.[11] Yet, until very recently, fasting was seldom even mentioned much less practiced. Even now, serious biblical fasting is exceedingly rare. To many modern believers, simple biblical teaching on fasting still sounds extreme and unusual. We know beyond question that fasting was a common practice for the first four hundred years after Christ's resurrection.

(8) *Past prayer meetings were often characterized by great fervency and inspiring testimonies.* Believers really expected mighty answers to their prayers. As a result, their meetings were anything but dead and formal! Glorious public testimonies ignited faith and spurred whole congregations to ever greater depths of prayer. By contrast, today's prayer meetings are often routine and uninspiring.

As we consider the dynamic prayer meetings of the past, is it any wonder that God so moved in previous centuries? However, for the sake of accuracy and balance, let me state clearly that not all prayer meetings of past were powerful and vibrant. Certainly there were periods when past prayer meetings became dead and formal. Yet, in every generation that experienced a mighty move of God, the common denominator was dynamic corporate prayer!

Friends, it really doesn't take a genius to see that most modern prayer

Biblical Patterns for Powerful Church Prayer Meetings

meetings are extremely different from the churches of the great awakenings. But, believers, we should take hope. Through God's grace our prayer meetings can change! Indeed, there are practical ways we can return to powerful prayer meetings without abandoning today's important activities and ministry organizations. Before I describe how prayer meetings can change, we must further consider why prayer meetings declined in the first place.

Why Did Churches Abandon Powerful Prayer Meetings?

There is absolutely no question that most churches have abandoned the dynamic prayer patterns of revival generations. The question is, "Why did it happen?" Certainly prayer patterns didn't change overnight and it is unlikely that changes were intentional. In general, five factors have contributed to the decline of modern church prayer meetings.

(1) *As church programs and organizational activities became more numerous, Wednesday nights took on many purposes besides prayer.* As a result, congregations began to divide into many different groups with a wide variety of activities. Too often it is to conserve time for people who feel they are too busy to pray. In this pattern, we see a tragic example of the good becoming a substitute for the best.

*As a side note, let me emphasize that activities and organizations do not have to be the enemy of prayer! Though it may require some schedule changes, there is certainly no reason we cannot do both organizational activities and powerful prayer.

Some churches take one Wednesday night per month or quarter to suspend all activities and conduct powerful church-wide prayer meetings. With this pattern, all organizations still get strong emphasis and yet at least once a month we have an awesome church-wide prayer meeting! (In previous generations, prayer meetings were often held monthly.)

Still other churches establish a separate night each week to do nothing but pray. (This is an excellent approach because it provides a vibrant weekly prayer meeting for our more serious intercessors.) When we are serious about something, there is always a way to do it! We now return our attention to why prayer meetings changed.

(2) *Because of a variety of midweek activities, modern prayer meetings were pushed into ever shorter time slots.* Dynamic prayer meetings gradually disappeared as less and less time was allotted for actual

prayer. Many churches simply stopped making enough time for serious encounters with God. In a push for brevity and convenience many churches unwittingly scheduled God right out of their midst. (It is utterly unrealistic to think we can experience fervent, mountain-moving prayer in tiny micro-managed time slots.)

(3) *Because many pastors were not experienced or confident in leading prayer meetings, it was natural to substitute other activities in its place.* Furthermore, we must sadly note that many pastors simply do not view the prayer meeting as a genuine top priority. Churches must be led to practice serious prayer meetings and pastors must do the leading. It is inaccurate to say, "Modern congregations are just not interested in prayer." The reality is that few modern congregations have been led into fervent corporate prayer. Congregations will almost never rise above their pastor's personal priority, practice and leadership of prayer. In terms of prayer, as the pastor goes so goes the church.

(4) *As churches placed more and more focus on organizational programs, prayer was treated as a "side item" of lesser importance.* Such scheduling shows that many churches truly believe the right organization or program is of far greater importance than serious corporate prayer. (Our real priorities are always seen in what we do, not what we say.) Indeed, the printed schedules often reveal little or no importance placed on corporately meeting God in prayer. This practice not only demonstrates an excessive program reliance, it is offensive to God who demands that we humble ourselves in fervent prayer. God will never share His glory with men or programs! (Judges 7:2, 2 Corinthians 1:29)

(5) *By the mid 1950's, churches were three generations removed from a time when strong prayer meetings were the predominate practice.* By then, most church leaders and congregations had little experience or memory of what powerful church prayer meetings were actually like. As a result, prayer meetings gradually became a Bible lesson with a couple of brief prayers tacked on the end. By following this pattern, churches unknowingly abandoned the very essence of their spiritual power! Such a pattern is the exact opposite of the early church and every generation that experienced a great spiritual awakening.

Biblical Patterns for Powerful Church Prayer Meetings

According to 2 Chronicles 7:14, it is the depth of prayer and repentance among God's people that largely determines the spiritual condition of a nation. It is very possible that today's moral collapse is largely due to several generations that allowed prayer meetings to either weaken or disappear entirely. Tragically, it seems that many churches have promoted everything except the one thing that can bring the massive flood of God's power.

Now, friends, it isn't that we haven't had any prayer emphasis. Indeed we have had increased emphasis and talked about prayer quite a bit. Yet, the problem is one of definition and degree of practice. What many churches are calling a prayer ministry often lacks frequency and fervency. Also, the modern definition of a strong prayer meeting has so weakened that what many call a significant prayer meeting utterly pales beside those of the New Testament and revival generations. In practice, many churches have "defined prayer meetings down" to the point where they barely resemble the real thing. (Jeremiah 29:13; James 5:16)

Scripture and history clearly prove that fervent prayer is God's absolute requirement for sending mighty floods of awakening. Today we undoubtedly have the greatest strategies, the best trained ministers, and the most extensive organization in the history of Christianity. Yet, without dynamic church prayer meetings, we can be much like a fully-loaded Cadillac with a lawn mower engine. We've got all the bells and whistles but lack the nation-shaking power of past great awakenings.

Let's face it, if intense promotion, strong funding and new strategies could produce sweeping revival, Southern Baptists would have long since seen the greatest awakening in history! Yet in spite of a fifty-year flood of new programs, the nation has witnessed its worst spiritual collapse and our baptisms their worst stagnation. Without intense prayer, programs easily become man-centered rather than God-dependant. Clearly there is immediate need for a fundamental change in priority and practice. That change is a wide spread return to the very root of our power—the dynamic corporate prayer meeting! (In truth, that's just about the only thing we haven't tried.)

Thank God for encouraging signs that a change is under way! Through prayer, some are indeed returning to genuine humility and total God-dependence. Growing numbers are beginning to realize that we cannot just promote programs and throw in a little prayer on the side. As with the generations before us, fervent prayer must again become the foundational practice that saturates all we do. (Acts 1:14; 2:42; 4:31; 13:1; 1 Thessalonians 5:17) Today, we are blessed with key denominational leaders who are truly beginning to lead in this direction!

A New Day is Dawning!

There is encouraging evidence that growing numbers of churches are returning to God through prayer! For the last fifteen years we have witnessed a steady rise of church prayer ministries. (Though the vast majority of churches still do not have serious prayer ministries, increasing numbers are moving in that direction.)

Furthermore, we are seeing a rising level of prayer in our evangelism and missions strategies. As never before we are seeing missions strategies connected to serious prayer. The International and North American Mission Boards and LifeWay have all created special department to focus on prayer. Capable and godly men are assigned to this task. A variety of effective new prayer strategies are now available. Some state conventions have also committed funding and personnel to develop deeper levels of intercession. Exciting changes are indeed under way.

Perhaps most encouraging is the rising level of corporate prayer in some churches and associations. For the past five years there has been a significant rise in corporate prayer meetings which target revival, evangelism, missions and spiritual awakening. Though such meetings still involve only a small minority of churches, the number is growing rapidly.

Based on scripture and history, today's increasing prayer movement is the single greatest hope for a nationwide awakening in America. Without such prayer, there has never been a nationwide spiritual awakening. With such prayer, sweeping revival is the sure promise of Almighty God! (2 Chronicles 7:14) Even as I write these words, there is unprecedented development of prayer across several state conventions. Pastor, the crucial question is, "Are you a part of this growing movement of fervent church-wide prayer?" If not, this resource is designed to show how you can be!

An Unprecedented Step by State Conventions

In recent months, many state conventions are embracing simultaneous prayer meetings across entire states. This urgent call to prayer involves specific Wednesday nights in which every church is asked to give at least thirty to sixty minutes to pray specifically for revival and evangelism across America. These state-wide calls to prayer are unique in that they will not be mentioned once and then forgotten. The specific nights of prayer will be promoted heavily and every pastor will receive biblical resources with practical patterns for conducting powerful meetings. Because America's crisis is so urgent, the state-wide calls to prayer will also be urgent.

Church leader, since you are reading this resource, your state convention is probably one that has resolved to call its churches to prayer. With this call to prayer, we are fully facing the desperate condition of our society. Furthermore, we humbly acknowledge the total inadequacy of programs alone to stem the rushing tide of evil. In the spirit of 2 Chronicles 7:14, we seek to humble ourselves and return to prayer as generations before us.

This call to prayer is not just another promotion that will quickly come and go. Rather it is the deep determination to obey Jesus' command to become and remain a house of prayer. (Matthew 21:13) Believers, let us now join hands to become a people "saturated" with corporate prayer and evangelism. Toward this purpose, godly pastors will be the deciding factor.

The Essential Role of the Pastor

If the modern church is to return to biblical prayer meetings, one thing is certain—pastors are the absolute key! Beyond question, the rubber hits the road with the local pastor and his church. Certainly we all realize that a state or national convention cannot "decree" anything. Denominations can only suggest simultaneous prayer times and provide simple equipping resources. It is local pastors that will determine whether American churches really become houses of prayer. This resource is written in deepest recognition and respect for the essential role of the local pastor.

I write as a fellow pastor who has pastored many years in an extremely difficult setting. Over fifteen years ago I inherited a church in the midst of a catastrophic legal battle and huge moral scandal. Through intense prayer, we saw God preserve the church against overwhelming odds. We have seen corporate prayer impact our evangelism, discipleship, finances, and church unity in significant ways.

Biblical Patterns for Powerful Church Prayer Meetings

Based on scripture and history, corporate prayer is not only the biblical thing to do, it is the most practical thing we can do! Like nothing else, God uses prayer to release His supernatural presence in church discipleship, evangelism and missions. Beyond question, God's supernatural power is the desperate need of our day.

I want to give church leaders a strong word of encouragement and hope. By God's grace, any church can experience dynamic growth in its practice of prayer! Oh I know it's easy to think, "Other churches could grow in prayer, but not ours." Please know, there are several biblical patterns for prayer meetings, and there is surely one God will use in your church. Above all, don't be discouraged! Even if you have to take very small steps, God will mightily bless your efforts. Believe me, your church can experience deeper levels of prayer and you can experience God's presence in every area of your ministry! (If my church can, any church can.)

In Chapter Two, we will examine general biblical patterns for conducting powerful prayer meetings in local congregations. Chapter Three contains a description of "nine foundational principles" for dynamic church prayer meetings. You will soon see how any church can experience God through vibrant corporate prayer! (Jeremiah 29:13; Matthew 7:7)

Chapter Two
Four Practical Patterns for Powerful Prayer Meetings

Today more and more pastors are asking the question, "How can I lead my church to experience powerful prayer meetings that are biblical and balanced?" Indeed, every pastor knows the importance of considering the unique needs of his own congregation. What might work beautifully in one congregation could actually cause division in another.

In this chapter I provide a general description of four biblical patterns for dynamic church prayer meetings. However, please understand these are merely patterns and are not intended as "rigid programs" or "magic formulas." Neither do I imply that these are the only patterns God mightily uses. (In fact, a wonderful possibility is to alternate your format as God's Spirit directs.) This helps maintain a glorious sense of freshness and vitality in your meetings.

At this point I need to stress the importance of not becoming overly bound to a schedule or program. There has never been a great awakening in which people were rigidly enslaved to a clock! On the other hand, God's leaders are responsible to guide God's people in balanced, biblical prayer patterns. (After all, God never condones disorder or imbalance.) Our sample patterns are only listed to give leaders a general sense of how meetings might flow. In other words, learn from the patterns but do not be bound by them. My goal is a healthy balance between effective planning and God-led spontaneity.

Again, this resource is designed for practical help in all churches and not just those whose state conventions are calling united nights of prayer. If your state is calling for particular nights of united prayer, you will receive specific information concerning particular dates and special focus. Furthermore, the patterns in this chapter are written to encourage churches toward powerful prayer meetings each week and not just for times of special emphasis.

In describing the four patterns, I will begin with the more basic and move to some that are a little more advanced. With any of the patterns, the pastor can certainly incorporate additional Bible teaching or confession time as God leads. For each pattern I provide a sample format for prayer meetings approximately one hour in length. For thirty minute meetings, you would simply abbreviate the preliminary activities and reduce the number and length of prayer seasons. In longer meetings, you would extend the length of prayer seasons and subjects as God directs. While conducting any meeting, always be sensitive to the possibility God may lead you to adjust your focus or length. (Remember, prayer is a relationship, not a program!)

Pattern One: A Simple Meeting of Corporate and Individual Prayer
(Involves Little Prior Preparation)

A General Description: In this very simple pattern, prayer time alternates between corporate prayers and brief periods when participants are asked to pray silently (or softly). It's primary use is for shorter prayer meetings. This pattern may be a starting place for churches that have little experience with corporate prayer. It might also be used when congregations are extremely hesitant to pray aloud.

In preparation for the meeting the pastor (or prayer leader) should organize the key prayer subjects into related categories. Each major category will receive a focused period (or season) of prayer. When you have prayerfully chosen the major categories for prayer, list several specific requests (or needs) related to each category. Either distribute these lists to the congregation or be prepared to state the key needs before each season of prayer. (It is usually preferable to distribute specific requests.)

When you begin the first season of prayer, call attention to the category and briefly describe the specific requests. Give opportunity for the congregation to voice any additional concerns related to the subject. Keep the talking about the requests very brief. You are there to pray.

Either the pastor or a prayer leader may begin the first season of prayer by corporately praying for the key requests. He should then ask the congregation to take the next few moments to pray silently for all the key needs for that prayer category. (If you have written out all the prayer requests you can encourage people to use the prayer sheets as a guide.) Give the congregation a few moments (at least 4-6 minutes) to pray silently (or softly) for all the needs. Be sure to encourage the people to pray and not to just to sit in silence. (It is often effective to use soft instrumental music during the silent prayer times.) At the end of a few minutes of silence, ask for a volunteer to pray corporately for all the needs of that particular prayer season. If needed the pastor (or designated person) can pray a further prayer to conclude the season of prayer.

The pastor (or leader) that introduces the next subject and follows the same pattern throughout each prayer season. This simple pattern is extremely flexible. There are many ways to vary such a pattern by giving more or less time to either the silent or corporate prayers. Each congregation will choose its own subjects and the number of requests related to each. I have seen God mightily use this pattern in either brief or mid-length prayer meetings.

I recommend singing of hymns and choruses at strategic points of the prayer meeting. In any prayer meeting, you should strive for a smooth transition from one prayer season to the next. Avoid abrupt breaks and disruptions in the flow of the meeting. With a little experience, the congregation flow smoothly from worship into prayer and back to worship.

Pattern one is a simple approach that can be non-intimidating to congregations unaccustomed to corporate prayer. However, I urge pastors not to sell their congregations short! Church leaders are often surprised that congregations respond well to prayer meetings that are more advanced than pattern one. If we are to see sweeping revival, we can no longer settle for shallow levels of prayer.

Pattern Two: A Combined Corporate and Small Group Prayer Meeting
(Involves Some Prior Preparation)

A General Description: This meeting generally begins with a time of corporate prayer, continues with a major period of small group prayer and concludes with a time of corporate prayer. Of all the formats, I have found Pattern Two to be the most powerful and practical for a widest range of churches.

The initial corporate prayers can be led by one person or as many as four or five. After the initial corporate prayers of five to fifteen minutes, ask the congregation to gather in small groups of three to five people. The small groups can cluster in their seats or gather in groups around the altar. Ask the people to take the next 20 - 40 minutes to pray through all the specific requests on the prayer sheets. In this type of meeting, it is very important to have comprehensive prayer sheets. During the small group prayer time, encourage specific intercession for key kingdom issues such as lost people, evangelism, missions, revival and spiritual awakening.

When it is time to end the small group prayer time, the pastor (or leader) can signal an instrumentalist to softly play a few verses of a hymn. The verse alerts the groups to bring their praying to a close. The meeting then concludes with one or more persons leading corporate prayers that address all the key requests of the meeting. It is often effective to have everyone stand and join hands as the concluding prayer is offered. It can also be moving to end with songs of celebration or praise for God's mercy and power. In this manner, the meeting concludes in a powerful sense of anticipation, hope, and praise!

Be sensitive to those who desire further prayer. Encourage them to continue in prayer and provide a specific room or designated area for that purpose. (Many churches routinely quench the Holy Spirit by abruptly ending prayer while people still need to pray.)

In listing the following outlines, I debated about whether to include any specific times. I elected to do so to give leaders an approximate sense of the general flow of a meeting. However, I would never distribute such a time schedule to the general congregation. We want sensitivity to God's Spirit not preoccupation with a program.

A Sample Outline for Pattern Two
(Listed times are only examples and are not to be viewed as a rigid schedule)

7:00 p.m. - **Welcome and Opening Hymn or Choruses**

7:05 p.m. - **Brief Testimonies of Answered Prayer**

7:10 p.m. - **Scripture Reading, Opening Prayer and Cleansing:** Read scriptures that focus on God's power and mercy. Briefly share any insights or special instructions for the prayer time. The pastor (or layman) should lead an opening prayer and then ask participants to search their heart and confess any sin God brings to mind. Ask the people to quickly bow before God. Allow a few moments of silence for people to confess their sins to God. (Psalms 139:23-24; Psalm 66:18) *For a confession guide, check resources in the back.

7:20 p.m. - **Identification of Prayer Needs**: During this period, call attention to the various issues for prayer. Emphasize key subjects and encourage the congregation to use the prayer sheet as a general guide. In this way, intercession will be both focused and thorough.

7:25 p.m. - **Corporate Prayers**: Two or three people should lead in corporate prayers for the key subjects on the list. The prayer leaders can be pre-designated or this time can be left open for spontaneous prayers.

7:35 p.m. - **Release the congregation into extended small group prayer time**: During this time period, the groups pray through all the subjects as God's Spirit directs. (This primary prayer period is especially powerful for praying for the lost by name.)

7:55 p.m. - **Concluding Corporate Prayers**: Give opportunity for a few people to lead final prayers for the key issues of focus. During the final prayer (led by pastor or leader) you may have people stand and join hands or kneel around the altar. It is often effective to conclude the meeting with a song or verbal testimonies of praise. Be sure to make provision for those who may be led to continue in prayer beyond the regular time period.

Key Advantages of Pattern Two

(1) The congregation experiences a powerful balance between corporate and small group prayer.

(2) This pattern maximizes time spent in actual prayer.

(3) This approach maximizes group participation and affords everyone ample opportunity to pray aloud. With such a format, people tend to participate rather than merely observe.

(4) This type of meeting is simple and flows well. There is usually a strong sense that the meeting is Spirit-directed and God-focused. (When it is led properly, congregations will experience a strong degree of freedom and spontaneity.)

Potential Difficulties

(1) It is possible that some may be uncomfortable with the significant time in small group prayer. Some people could feel they are being put on the spot to pray verbally. (This problem is usually remedied by assuring people they can pray silently if they so choose.)

(2) Some people have little interest in praying for issues that do not directly affect their daily life. For such people, this kind of meeting will hold little interest. We must face the fact that increasing the prayer time may actually reduce attendance at some church prayer meetings. (However, in many other churches the attendance actually increases!)

In essence, we must decide which is more pleasing to God; to have churches with no prayer meetings, or to become houses of prayer even if some choose not to participate? To me it comes down to one simple question. "Do we really want to let prayerless people dictate whether or not we have vibrant church prayer meetings?" I hope our answer is no!

Pattern Three: A Simple Corporate Prayer Meeting
(Involves Some Prior Preparation)

A General Description: In this basic yet powerful meeting, participants simply pray aloud for a wide variety of requests. The vast majority of time is spent in spontaneous verbal intercession for various issues of concern. (Though of course, not everyone in the congregation is required to pray aloud.) This particular pattern is more effective in small to midsize churches. It often amazes pastors that their congregations respond well to this type of prayer meeting.

In preparation for the meeting, leaders should organize the prayer concerns into related categories with each receiving a focused period (or season) of prayer. Though you will certainly not pray through all categories in each meeting, you should at least be familiar with the ten kingdom issues that deserve frequent prayer. (For a thorough listing of kingdom issues for prayer, see page 42.)

In most prayer meetings you will choose only two to four major "categories" to receive a focused season of prayer. Related to each category, you should list several "specific" prayer requests and distribute the list to those who attend the meeting. You could also provide the lists for intercessors who are homebound. Effective weekly prayer sheets are invaluable toward strengthening the daily prayer lives of people in the congregation! Use discretion about listing the names of lost or backslidden people on a public prayer sheet. Consider using only first names. If you choose not to use written lists of requests, then clearly state the specific requests before each season of prayer. In that way your people will be able to remember the key issues for each season of prayer.

A Sample Outline and Description for Pattern Three

(Listed times and subjects are only approximate examples and should not be viewed as rigid patterns. Each church will choose times and subjects for their own seasons of prayer.)

7:00 p.m. - **Welcome and Opening Hymns or Choruses**

7:05 p.m. - **Brief Testimonies of Praise or Answered Prayer**

7:10 p.m. - **Scripture Reading and Spiritual Preparation.** Read scriptures which focus on God's power to answer prayer. (Mark 11:22-24; John 14:12-14; 1 John 5:14-15, etc.) Briefly share any necessary instructions for the prayer time. The pastor or prayer leader should then lead an opening prayer and ask people to privately confess any sin God brings to mind. Pause for several moments of silence to allow participants to search their hearts. (In longer meetings or solemn assemblies there can be ample time for in-depth or even public confession.) The opening prayer time should major on: (a) asking for God's forgiveness, and (b) asking for His power on the prayer meeting.

7:20 p.m. - **First Season of Prayer (For the Lost and Backslidden).** (1 Peter 3:9) Especially in smaller churches, prayers for the lost can be offered corporately. Encourage people to bring their prayer lists of lost people. (The pastor or prayer leader should also prepare a list of known lost people.) I suggest asking someone to begin this season with a corporate prayer for God's convicting power on the persons we lift before Him. Following the corporate prayer, ask people to pray spontaneously for lost people. They may pray aloud, silently, or in small groups. After several minutes a designated person or volunteer should lead in a corporate prayer to conclude this particular season of prayer.

Biblical Patterns for Powerful Church Prayer Meetings

7:35 p.m. - **Second Season of Prayer (For Missionaries, Church Ministries, Denominational Needs, Revival and Spiritual Awakening)**. Briefly call attention to specific needs in this crucial category. (The International and North American Mission Boards can supply specific mission requests.) Ask one or two persons to be prepared to voice corporate prayers for the various concerns. One of the designated persons will begin with a corporate prayer after which you encourage others to voice spontaneous prayers. Following several minutes of intercession one of the designated persons should ends the season with a corporate prayer. (For updated prayer requests from the North American Mission Board, call 800-554-PRAY or contact www.namb.net/prayer. For updated prayer requests from the International Mission Board, call 800-395-PRAY or contact www.IMB.org/pray.)

7:50 p.m. - **Third Season of Prayer (For the Sick & Bereaved)**. (James 5:15-16) This prayer season can be used for any "temporal need" (finances, job, etc.). In congregations that do not readily pray aloud, it is often helpful to pre-designate one or two spiritual people to begin and end each season with a corporate prayer. After the special needs are mentioned briefly, one of the designated persons begins with a corporate prayer. The pastor or leader then asks the people to enter a period of spontaneous prayer for the stated needs of that prayer season. Whether or not they come to the microphone depends on the size of the sanctuary and whether or not they can be easily heard. After several minutes of spontaneous prayers, one of the designated persons leads the closing prayer for this particular season. (In any meeting if no one prays spontaneously, the pastor or designated persons should go ahead and pray for all the needs of that particular prayer season.)

8:00 p.m. - **Concluding Prayer of Agreement** (Matthew 18:19). Pastor (or prayer leader) asks the congregation to stand and join hands (optional). He then leads in a concluding prayer that includes all of the prayer categories mentioned in the meeting. This prayer is offered in the expectant faith that answers are on the way. The final joint prayer is one of exuberant praise for God's mercy and power. It is often effective for congregations to sing songs of celebration just after the closing prayer, such as "To God Be The Glory" or "Victory in Jesus." Be sensitive to the possibility that some may want to share an insight or testimony after the concluding prayer. God often changes lives during the prayer meeting! Also encourage people to continue in prayer as God's Spirit leads them. You may want to provide an adjoining room or designated area for this purpose.

Pattern Four: Alternating Seasons of Corporate and Small Group Prayer
(Involves more prior preparation)

A General Description: This meeting is generally characterized by a fairly equal balance of corporate and small group prayer time. The congregation will be led through several seasons of prayer with corporate and small group prayer occurring in each season. Intercession flows freely from corporate to small group prayer as the congregation moves through various seasons of prayer. This format is usually more effective for longer prayer meetings and in congregations of greater size. Pattern Four takes a bit more coordination and planning.

Typically such meetings are characterized by four phases: (1) opening prayers, scripture reading and brief prayer instructions, (2) a period of praise (verbal testimonies, songs, choruses, quoted Bible verses of praise and prayers of thanksgiving), (3) a period of confession and cleansing (to prepare the congregation for prayer), (4) the primary time of intercession. Obviously in shorter meetings each phase will be limited. Since this type of meeting requires more coordination, I will provide a more detailed description of some practical steps.

Sample Steps for Pattern Four

Step One: After the opening prayer, briefly share scriptures that relate to key prayer principles. The amount of scripture largely depends on the planned length of the meeting. If an hour is scheduled, you could conduct a ten minute Bible lesson and still have significant time for prayer. Again, many churches find it helpful periodically to conduct an eight week series of brief Bible lessons in conjunction with the prayer time. Through this process, the congregation receives excellent prayer instruction as well as strong preparation for the prayer meeting. After all, weekly prayer meetings will never be stronger than the individual prayer lives of those who participate! An important goal of the weekly meeting is to grow believers to far deeper levels of prayer. This is attainable by combining brief prayer teaching with the significant periods of actual prayer.

Step Two: Move into a period of praise and thanksgiving. Though there are many options for the time of praise, two seem to be the most effective. First, ask the congregation to offer verbal prayers of thanks and praise. When congregations get accustomed to spontaneous praise, it is amazing how freely they voice their prayers. After the people have voice prayers of praise, the pastor (or lay leader) offers a powerful corporate prayer of praise and worship to God. Second, ask for verbal testimonies of praise and answered prayer. After some have shared, lead the congregation in a prayer of praise and thanksgiving.

*If the testimonies begin to go too long, gently bring it to a close so as not to compromise the time for intercession.

*If no one testifies aloud, the pastor (or someone appointed) proceeds with a corporate prayer of praise and thanksgiving.

Step Three: Continue with a time of confession and spiritual preparation. (Proverbs 28:13; 1 John 1:9) A vital key to a powerful meeting is leading people in spiritual preparation for prayer. Some may not have the opportunity (or inclination) to properly prepare for prayer beforehand. For this reason conduct a period of silent reflection during which you ask the people to confess any known sin. Just a few minutes of reflection can allow God to bring obvious sins to the minds of the people. Though this is not an in-depth spiritual cleansing, it is enough to help some of your people to get on praying ground. (In two hour prayer meetings, there is more time for in-depth confession and repentance.) I strongly encourage more thorough cleansing through periodic church-wide solemn assemblies.

Step Four: Lead the congregation through specific seasons of intercession for key prayer subjects. As the prayer leader introduces the subjects of each prayer season, he should briefly state some of the key points. (Do not go into great detail or launch into a sermon as this will diminish the time for prayer.) Encourage the congregation to use the prayer lists for guidance in the seasons of prayer. The leader then asks the people to gather in groups of three to five as they prepare for intercession. Some may want to stay seated in groups while others might gather at the altar. The following guidelines will help this time go smoothly.

Sample Outlines for Pattern Four
(Listed times are only examples and are not intended as rigid schedules)

A Sample One-Hour Prayer Meeting

6:50 p.m. - Prelude of Worship Music

7:00 p.m. - Welcome, Introduction and Opening Prayer

7:05 p.m. - Choruses, Scripture reading, Confession, and Preparation for Prayer

7:15 p.m. - Season of Prayer for Sick, Bereaved, and other Crises (in corporate and small groups)

7:30 p.m. - Season of prayer for the Lost, Unchurched, Church Ministries, Missionaries (in corporate and small groups)

7:45 p.m. - Season of Prayer for Revival and Spiritual Awakening (in corporate and small groups)

8:00 p.m. - Closing Prayer (corporate)

(Each week you could rotate some of the categories of focus. In this manner you will cover a complete range of issues every four to six weeks.) One advantage of this approach is its flexibility for churches of all sizes. I have seen God mightily anoint this pattern in prayer meetings all the way from 30 to 3,000 people. The inclusion of appropriate music and worship is especially important in this type of meeting.

In some churches, Pattern Four can lend itself to meetings of greater fervency and spontaneity. In churches mature enough for extended prayer, I suggest you have fewer seasons (or breaks) and simply release the people for longer periods of spontaneous prayer. Some past revivals witnessed meetings in which the entire congregation prayed yet, with a beautiful sense of order. For a detailed examination of twelve different formats for corporate prayer and worship see *A Comprehensive Guide to Church and Small Group Prayer Meetings*. (See Resources for Further Reference on page 48.) Indeed, there are many ways to experience powerful intercession! The key is close sensitivity to the Holy Spirit within a healthy framework of biblical balance and order.

Biblical Patterns for Powerful Church Prayer Meetings

A Sample Two-Hour Prayer Meeting
(Listed times are not rigid)

6:45 p.m. - Prelude of Worship Music

7:00 p.m. - Welcome, Introduction and Opening Prayer

7:05 p.m. - Period of Congregational Worship and Special Soloists

7:15 p.m. - Season of Testimonies and Prayers of Praise

7:25 p.m. - Soloist or Group Worship Song

7:30 p.m. - Scripture Reading for Confession and Repentance

7:35 p.m. - Prayers of Confession and Repentance (Congregation is lead through deep spiritual cleansing.) A detailed congregational confession guide is available in *A Comprehensive Guide to Corporate Prayer in Churches and Small Groups*. (See list at the back of this resource.)

7:50 p.m. - Songs of Praise for God's Cleansing

7:55 p.m. - Reading of Prayer Promises

8:00 p.m. - Season of Prayer for Crises and Personal Needs (corporate and small groups)

8:15 p.m. - Season of Prayer for Lost, Unchurched, and Local Church Needs (corporate and small groups)

8:30 p.m. - Season of Prayer for the City, for Regional Revival, for Missionaries and Denominational Initiatives (corporate and small groups)

8:45 p.m. - Season of Prayer for Revival and Awakening (corporate and small groups)

9:00 p.m. - Closing Prayers and Worship (corporate)

Practical Guidelines for Seasons of Prayer in Small Groups

(1) Encourage the prayer groups to pray aloud but always allow the freedom for some individuals to pray silently.

(2) Encourage the people to pray loud enough to be heard by their group but not necessarily by the whole church. This will help keep the meeting decent and in order.

(3) When it is time to end each season of prayer, an instrumentalist should softly play one or two verses of an appropriate hymn. Usu-

ally the prayer leader can simply nod to the instrumentalist when he senses it is time to end each season of prayer. I suggest a bare minimum of eight to ten minutes for each season. (More is usually better) You do not want the seasons of prayer to be so brief that no one really has a chance to pray! The appropriate length of prayer seasons usually depends on the number of subjects for each season. Another important key is to provide many specific requests on your prayer sheet. In this way, people will not run out of prayer needs. (Although we should never give them the idea they can only pray from the printed list.)

(4) As the people end their small group prayers, the leader (or one appointed) should voice a corporate prayer for the issues addressed in that particular season. At this point you are ready to move immediately to the next season of prayer.

(5) The prayer leader briefly shares the focus of the next season, calls attention to the prayer guides and again releases the people into small group prayer. An appropriate Bible verse might be quoted. Follow the same pattern throughout each season of prayer. (Be carefully not to spend excessive time introducing the different prayer seasons.)

(6) The prayer leader closes the meeting with a final prayer of praise for God's anticipated answers. During the concluding prayer ask the entire congregation to stand or gather at the altar. It is especially moving if the worship leader closes by leading songs such as "God is so Good," "To God be the Glory," or "Victory in Jesus."

Practical Pointers for Any Corporate Prayer Meeting

1. It is by no means always necessary to designate people to lead corporate prayers. Congregations can leave prayer meetings open to the spontaneous promptings of God's Spirit. In churches where people readily pray aloud, the spontaneous approach is certainly more effective. However in many churches, prayer meetings may flow smoother if some are prepared to give prayer leadership at strategic points. It is not unspiritual to ask godly people to prepare to lead prayer at a weekly meeting.

2. When you open the floor for spontaneous prayers, you may want to limit that to three or four people for each prayer season. Otherwise you can easily spend all your time on one subject or fall into a repetitive pattern. After a designated person opens with a corporate prayer, ask two or three others to voice spontaneous prayers as God's Spirit directs. In this way, there is freedom for spontaneous prayer yet the spiritual leaders still have general direction of the meeting. However, there may be times you sense God's leading to focus the whole meeting on only one or two urgent subjects. Again, the guiding principle is close sensitivity to the Spirit of God. We should avoid getting so set on a schedule that we deny God's Spirit the freedom to lead!

3. It is not necessary to ask different people to lead each corporate prayer. In some smaller churches, the pastor and one or two others may be the only ones who are comfortable to pray verbally. Even if the pastor is the only corporate intercessor, churches can still have powerful prayer meetings. If necessary, the pastor can pray for each category and ask the congregation to join him silently. (In historic awakenings, lengthy pastoral prayers were not uncommon.)

4. There is no set number of subjects you must cover in the prayer meeting. In fact, if you conduct fewer seasons of prayer you are not as rushed and can focus more intensely on each subject. Fewer seasons of prayer are especially important if you only schedule a thirty minute prayer time. The length and number of seasons are largely dictated by the planned length of the prayer meeting. In our examples, I have mostly described one hour prayer meetings. Obviously in shorter meetings it is necessary to adjust both the length and number of prayer seasons.

5. Choose permanent subjects that are addressed each week and other subjects that rotate from week to week. (However, we should never be bound to a program if God's Spirit leads in another direction.) In this way you thoroughly cover all key kingdom issues at least every six weeks. Modern congregations must learn to intercede for the full range of kingdom issues. For permanent subjects I suggest lost people, missionaries, crisis needs, revival and spiritual awakening.

Quick Answers to Commonly Asked Questions

Though we cannot cover all questions in this chapter, we can address a few of the most common. The following six questions are some of the most frequently asked.

1. **How can we conduct powerful church-wide prayer meetings without abandoning other crucial activities and ministries?**
   - By rescheduling some activities to times other than Wednesday night.
   - By extending the amount of time we are at church on Wednesday nights.
   - By scheduling a special church-wide prayer meeting monthly, bi-quarterly, or quarterly. (On this night other activities will be canceled and everyone will be in the prayer meeting.)
   - By scheduling an entirely different night in which you do nothing but pray. Don't worry about the size of the crowd. The serious intercessors will come. Such meetings can be of greater length and intensity.
   - By determining that coporate prayer is commanded by our Lord and must have priority.

2. **How can we motivate people to attend Wednesday night prayer meetings?**
   - By asking God to grant your people a spiritual hunger to seek His face. (After all, we cannot motivate anyone to pray.)
   - By consistent preaching and teaching on the importance of church-wide corporate prayer.
   - By consistently promoting the prayer meeting as a major priority
   - By planning inspiring and uplifting elements in the prayer meeting (testimonies, music, etc.)
   - By sharing testimonies of how God is answering the prayers of those who attend. (Share brief prayer testimonies in the Sunday morning service.)
   - By emphasizing that people will learn to pray by attending the prayer meeting.
   - By emphasizing that people will experience great spiritual growth through the prayer meeting.

- By modeling significant corporate prayer in the worship service.
3. **How do we help people to look outward in their praying?**
    - By providing specific written prayer requests for a full range of kingdom issues.
    - By teaching them how to be effective intercessors.
    - By testimonies of what happens when we pray for others.
    - By scheduling seasons of prayer that focus on a variety of specific issues.
4. **How do we maintain focus in the prayer meeting?**
    - By providing comprehensive prayer lists for each category of focus.
    - By utilizing "seasons of prayer" to address the various issues.
    - By effective leadership and preparation from the pastor or prayer leader.
    - By asking certain people to pray for specific issues.
5. **How do we keep prayer meetings fresh and spontaneous?**
    - By asking God's direction as you carefully plan each prayer meeting.
    - By varying the flow of the meeting as God's Spirit directs.
    - By utilizing personal testimonies and reports of answered prayer.
    - By gathering the staff to ask God's blessing on the prayer meetings.
6. **How do we get people to pray out loud?**
    - By consistently encouraging people to pray out loud.
    - By emphasizing the "sincerity" of prayer rather than how it "sounds."
    - By assigning various people to pray out loud. (Over time, they will come to feel more comfortable.)
    - By periodic scripture lessons that teach people how to pray.

Summation

The possibilities for exciting prayer meetings are almost endless! Again, the crucial factors are thorough preparation and close sensitivity to the Spirit of God. Yet, for too long we have treated the prayer meeting with profound carelessness. Fervent, church-wide prayer has been replaced by a myriad of substitutes. What should be the very engine and power source of our churches is often reduced to a sterile formality that few attend.

By our actions, we have in effect told God, "We really don't need your supernatural presence and power; just bless our programs." Believers, we have followed this path at terrible spiritual cost to our nation and to many of our churches. Yet, it is not too late to turn back to God in fervent prayer!

God has shaken our land in the past and He can surely do it again. Pastors, I won't try to tell you that dynamic prayer meetings will happen effortlessly. They won't! Churches never develop powerful biblical prayer meetings by accident. Indeed, there is nothing that Satan will oppose more than your commitment to lead your church to God in fervent prayer. It definitely takes determined leadership and consistent preparation by key church leaders. But it can be done and the awesome results are well worth the effort! It is my urgent prayer that God will use this booklet to grant His leaders the burning desire and practical skills to reclaim Christ's church as a "house of prayer." The very soul of our nation depends on it!

The next chapter contains foundational principles that are essential to powerful prayer meetings. While I am certainly not trying to over complicate the prayer meeting, there are certain principles that are vital to building dynamic, biblical encounters with God. As you read Chapter Three, ask God to give you the vision for a glorious new day of prayer in your congregation. Without a vision, the people perish! (Proverbs 29:18)

Chapter Three
Foundational Principles for Powerful Prayer Meetings

In this chapter, I describe nine principles that are foundational to meeting God in powerful prayer meetings. These principles are based on God's changeless patterns from scripture and history. At the end of each section, you will find a question to help you evaluate the present strength of your own meeting. The evaluation questions serve as a "checklist" to help congregations prepare for powerful encounters with God. Above all, do not be overwhelmed by what you read and please do not think you have to embrace all nine steps before you can experience powerful prayer meetings!

While conducting scores of prayer conferences, I have seen God mightily bless even the tiniest first steps of churches seeking to strengthen their prayer meetings. Be assured that our merciful Father will take you right where you are and patiently lead your church in a glorious new relationship with Himself. After all, the prayer meeting is not about formulas and formats, it is a dynamic encounter with God Himself! As you read the following pages, ask God to reveal simple ways to revolutionize your own church prayer gatherings.

Foundational Steps to Powerful Midweek Prayer Meetings

(1) **Give Prayerful Planning to the Weekly Prayer Meeting.** Churches always show their real priorities by what they seriously plan, organize, and promote. Today, where prayer meetings exist at all, they are often carelessly planned and under promoted. Brethren, when we give such haphazard attention to the prayer meeting, we are speaking volumes about our true view of prayer. Thank God this pattern is changing!

Growing numbers of churches involve musicians, lay leaders, and the entire staff in planning dynamic weekly prayer meetings. Though this takes work and preparation, such efforts make a huge difference in the churches that take prayer seriously. However, I again state that planning should not be so rigid as to lose sensitivity to God's Spirit. Your planning must leave room for the spontaneous response of God's people. Yet please don't despair! God will surely lead you in the proper balance of planning and spontaneity.

Evaluation Question: What does your present level of planning suggest about your true view of the prayer meeting?

(2) **Promote the Weekly Prayer Meeting as a Genuine Top Priority.** According to Jeremiah 29:13, our attitude toward prayer must be one of high intensity and top priority. "And ye shall seek me, and find me, when ye shall search for me with all your heart." Churches seldom develop dynamic prayer meetings until prayer an actual becomes top priority. (Such a strong emphasis on the weekly prayer meeting will require a major change in the promotional practice of most churches.)

To help congregations gain a priority view of the prayer meeting, I suggest a series of eight brief Bible studies that teach the importance of corporate intercession. For a collection of these studies, check the resource *Bible Studies that Prepare for Prayer Meetings* by Gregory Frizzell.

It is absolutely vital that we teach modern congregations the central role of prayer in all great revivals and in all true evangelism. Until congregations fully grasp the importance of corporate intercession, they will continue to view prayer meetings as optional and unimportant.

Evaluation Question: Does your congregation promote the prayer meeting as a major priority?

(3) **View the Prayer Meeting as a "Relationship Encounter" with God.** (Matthew 6:7) "But when you pray, use no vain repetitions, as the heathen do; for they think that they will be heard for their much speaking." As humans, we have a tragic tendency to so tightly orchestrate events that there is little opportunity for a genuine encounter with God. In fact, if we're not careful, we can treat a prayer meeting as just another program to implement. We must remember that spiritual power is not in some rigid prayer format, but in a right relationship with God. Remember, God does not answer prayer, He answers persons who are in right relationship with Himself. (After all, the Pharisees prayed all the time, but they had no relationship with God.)

Without a strong focus on God Himself, we can actually program the life out of a prayer meeting! We avoid this by primarily viewing the prayer meeting as a relationship experience with God rather than merely an event to program. In our prayer meeting, the primary goal is to make significant time for people to experience a genuine, spontaneous encounter with God. Church leader, be assured if you seek God's direction, He will guide you into balanced, biblical meetings in which your people truly encounter God.

Evaluation Question: Is your prayer meeting so tightly structured that there is no room for the spontaneous leadership of the Holy Spirit?

(4) **Use the Weekly Prayer Meeting to Grow Your People in Intercession.** (Luke 11:1) "One of his disciples said unto him, Lord, teach us to pray, as John also taught his disciples." We must face the fact that most modern believers do not know how to pray effectively. The weekly prayer meeting is the crucial place to teach them! After all, we do not primarily learn to pray by reading books or attending conferences; we learn to pray by praying! If congregations hear weekly prayer teaching, see prayer demonstrated, and then experience it themselves, they will soon learn to meet God on a totally different level. Nothing teaches people to pray like praying and hearing others pray!

The prayer meeting is also the ideal time to give your people detailed prayer lists for key issues. Unfortunately, many churches have prayer sheets that are totally inadequate. An effective prayer sheet should contain several specific requests for each major category of prayer. (Under an upcoming point I will further describe the ten essential categories for effective prayer lists.)

By providing comprehensive prayer lists, we not only teach believers how to intercede, we deliver churches from the tragic practice of praying mostly for health concerns. In this way, believers move toward an outward kingdom focus rather than one that is inward and temporal. Effective prayer lists not only strengthen the weekly prayer meeting, they lead people to more focused prayer in their daily quiet times.

Evaluation Question: Does your church use the prayer meeting to deepen the prayer life of its people?

(5) Schedule Significant Prayer Time in the Weekly Meeting. (Matthew 26:40) "What, could you not watch with me one hour?" Though many churches still call Wednesday nights a prayer meeting, actual prayer is usually the least thing done. Wednesday night meetings typically consist of greetings, songs, announcements, a Bible devotion, and maybe five to seven minutes for prayer. (And most of those few minutes are spent discussing the prayer requests!)

It is all too common for people to spend so much time talking about prayer requests that almost no time is spent in prayer. As a result, very few churches experience anything that even remotely resembles the prayer meetings of the early church or any of the Great Awakenings. This could well be the biggest reason baptism ratios have (so seriously) declined over the past fifty years.

Modern churches must rethink the amount of time allotted for the weekly prayer meeting. Unfortunately, a great number of churches have gone to a thirty minute schedule and by the time they finish the greetings, songs, announcements, Bible teaching, and lists of requests, there might be five minutes for actual prayer. I am not saying you cannot have a meaningful thirty minute prayer meeting, indeed you can if you are prepared to minimize other activities and maximize the time in prayer.

Please further note that I am not saying that sharing God's Word is somehow less important than prayer. In fact, I encourage some brief sharing of scripture in the prayer meeting. (Though, the primary focus of the prayer meeting must be actual time in prayer!)

I strongly suggest that you schedule at least forty-five minutes to an hour for your weekly prayer meeting. In the first ten to twelve minutes, you could teach key scriptures and even allow a time for testimonies of answered prayer. After that, you can still devote a full thirty to forty minutes strictly to prayer.

Regardless of the length of a prayer meeting, the guiding principle is to schedule most of your time for actual prayer. In most churches this will require major changes, but, friend, believe me, the results will be worth it a million times over!

Evaluation Question: In your church prayer meetings, what percentage of the time is actually spent in prayer? Is that enough to really call your church a house of prayer?

(6) **Focus Prayer Mostly on Issues that are Eternal Rather than Temporal.** (Ezekiel 22:30) "And I sought for a man among them, that should make up the hedge, and stand in the gap before me for the land, that I should not destroy it: but I found none." In most churches, what little time is spent in prayer, is focused almost entirely on physical and temporal needs. Tragically this means that our prayer focus is almost totally inward and temporal rather than outward and eternal.

While God is certainly concerned about physical needs, they are not His top priority. After all, which is of greater urgency to God, the salvation of an eternal soul or someone getting over a minor health problem? Which is of higher kingdom urgency, a sweeping revival in America or raising enough funds to carpet a fellowship hall?

The Father's heart is broken when we endlessly major on temporal concerns while our world is going to hell! Yet, with just a little planning, your church can achieve a healthy balance between eternal and temporal prayer concerns.

Evaluation Question: What percentage of your prayer meeting is actually focused on eternal kingdom issues? (Such as lost people, missionaries, evangelism efforts, revival in the church, etc.)

(7) **Lead the Congregation to Identify and Pray for the Key Kingdom Issues.** Under the previous point I emphasized the importance of praying for issues that are "eternal" rather than merely "temporal." In referring to eternal issues I prefer the term "key kingdom issues." But what is a key kingdom issue? I define it as follows: A key kingdom issue is one that directly relates to the spread of God's kingdom (evangelism and missions) and the spiritual growth of God's people (life-changing discipleship and revival).

The sad truth is that most churches cannot even name the key kingdom issues (much less effectively intercede for them). I am deeply convinced that churches must not only identify key kingdom issues but regularly intercede for them. With just a little awareness and planning, the midweek prayer meeting can produce a flood of spiritual power for the kingdom issues of our day.

Biblical Patterns for Powerful Church Prayer Meetings

So what are the "key kingdom issues" that deserve consistent intercession at prayer meetings. The following ten are some of the most crucial:

1. Specific confession and repentance from personal and corporate sin
2. Lost people and backslidden individuals
3. Sweeping revival and spiritual awakening
4. Missionaries, mission initiatives and unreached people groups
5. Specific church needs and ministry initiatives
6. Key denominational needs, ministries and leaders
7. Government, educational and cultural leaders
8. Sick, bereaved, widowed, orphaned, financial needs, etc.
9. Prayer for God to raise up many soul winners, pastors, teachers, missionaries, etc.
10. Prayer for persecuted believers

When churches identify and consistently pray for a full range of kingdom priorities, their spiritual impact quickly explodes many fold. After all, a church's prayer power will only be as great as its prayer focus. Remember, if intercession is to be biblical and powerful, it must be (a) consistent and (b) focused on matters of strategic kingdom importance.

It is tragic that so many churches pray with such a narrow band of focus. The corporate prayer life of most churches is tragically limited and shallow. It is extremely important that pastors lead congregations to grow up in the practice of mature, biblical prayer. Though it does take a little planning and preparation, we can lead our churches to pray regularly for the major kingdom issues. The results will be astounding!

For time reasons, most churches will not pray for every kingdom issue in each prayer meeting. I encourage pastors to choose two to four major issues to cover in each prayer meeting. At God's direction you can vary your focus from week to week. By alternating the weekly prayer focus, churches can easily pray for all kingdom issues every four to six weeks.

Another important advantage is the ability to help congregations pray for key kingdom issues in far greater depth. For each prayer subject, I suggest that you list several specific needs. It is vital to provide congregations with specific needs around which to focus their intercession. In this manner many believers would learn to incorporate the key kingdom issues into their personal intercession. This one practice could revolutionize the prayer power of churches and individual believers!

Evaluation Question: Does your church regularly intercede for all of the major kingdom issues? Do you provide your people with specific prayer needs related to each kingdom priority?

(8) **Schedule Additional Prayer Meetings for Your More Fervent Intercessors.** (James 5:16) "The effectual fervent prayer of a righteous man availeth much." A wise guideline for the Wednesday meeting is to develop strong prayer patterns, yet patterns that are not so extensive as to eliminate the vast majority of participants. For your more serious intercessors, it is crucial to offer additional prayer meetings of greater intensity and length. In many churches, growing numbers of people are yearning to go to deeper levels of prayer and we must provide the opportunity.

In my own church, the Wednesday night meeting includes various seasons of powerful prayer yet, this meeting is not extensive or overwhelming. For this reason, the majority of our people still feel able to participate. However, we conduct an additional weekly prayer meeting for those willing to pray at length for lost people, for needs in the church, and for revival in America.

The additional prayer meeting is open to everyone and is usually held Sunday nights after church or some night during the week. Though fewer numbers attend this meeting, it is characterized by much greater power and phenomenal results always spring from this smaller group!

Evaluation Question: Does your church have at least one weekly prayer meeting that intensely targets lost people, revival in the church, and spiritual awakening in America?

(9) **Promote the Weekly Meeting as a Time of Joy and Life-Changing Power.** (John 16:24) "Hitherto have you asked nothing in my name: ask, and ye shall receive, that your joy may be full." When a church conducts powerful corporate prayer meetings, there will be many answered prayers and much reason for rejoicing! It is

often appropriate to begin prayer meetings with a time of sharing answered prayers. Absolutely nothing fills people with joy and prepares them to pray like hearing recent answers from God.

When churches approach prayer meetings expecting to meet God, they quickly discover that real prayer meetings are not dry and dead! Music and worship are especially powerful toward enhancing the life of a prayer meeting. If you choose songs that uplift and foster an atmosphere of expectancy, your midweek prayer meeting will become an incredibly vibrant service! When churches promote prayer meetings as a powerful life-changing event, far more people will attend.

Evaluation Question: Is your prayer meeting a time of joyful anticipation or is it a dull formality?

Again, please do not be overwhelmed by the list of nine principles of powerful prayer meetings. At its heart, the prayer meeting is wonderfully simple and God will lead you step by step to greater congregational prayer. We should also remember that no congregation can be forced to pray beyond their maturity level. As pastors lovingly and patiently lead their people to ever deeper levels of prayer, each shepherd will wisely discern what is best for his own flock. With God's grace and consistent effort, it can be done!

I pray every reader has received a glorious vision of meeting God through a new day of prayer in your church. Beyond question, it is God's will for your church to become "saturated" in prayer. (Matthew 21:13, Mark 11:17) It is almost certain that serious prayer patterns will be followed by increased evangelism, missions and revival in your church. Without such prayer, sweeping spiritual awakenings virtually never occur. With such prayer, God shakes whole nations! May God help us settle for nothing less than all of Himself. After all, prayer is not about getting blessed, it is about a far greater relationship with God. May God grant us a heart that ever seeks after Him!

Conclusion
A Pivotal Moment in History

As we consider moral trends of the past fifty years, we must ask ourselves the sobering question, "What will America be like in ten years if present trends continue?" As we ponder this question, one thing is obvious—we do not want to find out! More and more, people are realizing that a huge spiritual awakening is the only hope for our society. It is also essential for the cleansing and revitalization of Christ's church.

Thank God we have scripture and history to prove that God can send sweeping revival. Yet one fact is beyond question, God's primary pattern is a major return to corporate prayer, deep repentance, and fervent evangelism. With this fact in mind, we are all faced with a decision of enormous consequence.

The Decision Now Before Us

Jesus' words from Mark 11:17 leave no room for doubt about His will for the Church. "My house shall be called a house of prayer for all nations." At this point in our collective and personal journey, each of us will make a decision about whether we continue with business as usual or truly become a house of prayer.

In essence, your decision will be one of four responses. (1) You may decide that your church and personal prayer life is exactly where it needs to be and you need no growth. (2) You may decide that fervent corporate prayer is really not important and you sense no need for change. (3) You may sense a real need to go deeper in prayer but you are not going to act now. (In truth, this is a choice not to respond to God's voice.) (4) You may sense God telling you to make an immediate commitment and are now prepared to obey Him fully in prayer.

For many (including myself), number four is the response God seeks and is the only response worth of Him. May God help us grasp the extreme urgency of the hour and the importance of our decision to seek His face. For America and for many churches, it is now or never! Each of us must now make a decision about seeking God in fervent prayer. It is not a matter we can ignore. Dear believer, the eyes of God are upon you this moment and He has awesome blessings for those who seriously pray! *He now awaits your answer.* **What will it be?**

Notes

1. J. William Bennett, *The Index of Leading Cultural Indications* (New York: Broadway Books, 1999), 47-87.

2. U.S. Department of Justice; *Bureau of Justice Statistics, The Uniform Crime Report of the Federal Bureau of Investigation*, December 1999.

3. Michael Medved, *Hollywood vs. America* (New York: Harper Perenniel, 1992), 75-78.

4. Ibid., 79-81.

5. Research Department, North American Mission Board, Alpharetta, GA 1999.

6. G. Thomas Holbrooks, *Encyclopedia of Southern Baptists*, s.v. "Prayer Meetings." (Nashville: Broadman Press, 1982).

7. W. Charles Deweese, *Prayer in Baptist Life, A Historical Survey* (Nashville: Broadman Press, 1986), 29.

8. H. Brian Edwards, *Revival! A People Saturated with God* (Durham, England: Evangelical Press, 1990), 82-85.

9. Deweese, 99.

10. Edwards, 119-122.

11. Deweese, 49.

Resources for Further Reference

A Comprehensive Guide to Church and Small Group Prayer Meetings by Gregory Frizzell.

Bible Studies That Prepare for Prayer Meetings by Gregory Frizzell.

How to Develop an Evangelistic Church Prayer Ministry by Gregory Frizzell.

(The above listed books will be published in mid-2000. For pre-published material or other information, contact Dr. Frizzell at the address below.)

Local Associations and United Prayer: "Keys to the Coming Revival" by Gregory Frizzell, 1996.

A House of Prayer: "Prayer Ministries in Your Church" LifeWay Press, 1999. Compiled by John Franklin.

Biblical Patterns for Powerful Church Prayer Meetings
Fresh Wind, Fresh Fire by Jim Cymbala.

A Prayer Guidebook for Associations and Churches by Thomas Wright. (North American Mission Board or LifeWay Stores.) Available late 2000.

Prayer in Baptist Life by Charles W. Deweese. (Broadman Press, Nashville, TN), 1986.

Revival: "A People Saturated with God" by Brian H. Edwards, (Evangelical Press, Durham, England), 1990.

Revival Fire by Wesley Duewel, (Zondervan Publishing House, Grand Rapids, Michigan), 1995.

To schedule conferences on church prayer ministries, evangelistic praying, or developing powerful prayer meetings, contact:

Gregory Frizzell
3800 N. May Ave.
Oklahoma City, OK 73112
405-942-3800
gfrizzell@earthlink.net

John Franklin
LifeWay Christian Ministries
27 Ninth Ave N
Nashville, TN 37234
www.lifeway.com

Tim Bearden
Tennessee Baptist Convention
5001 Maryland Way
Brentwood, TN 37024
www.tnbaptist.org

Chris Schofield
North American Mission Board
4200 N. Point Pkwy
Alpharetta, GA 30022-4176
www.namb.net

Rob Finley
Prayer Resources
PO Box 569
Union City, TN 38281-0569
www.prayerresources.org